WORDS TO LIVE BY

Michael Gunn

ISBN: 1439256977
ISBN-13: 9781439256978

I would like to first give honor to God for giving me this talent. Also, to my parents Booker T. and Elizabeth Gunn for instilling strong family values and an entrepreneur spirit of never giving up on your dreams. They are looking down from heaven with smiles on their faces. Thanks to my brother Robert Gunn for always challenging me! Thanks to my sister Diane, and brothers John, Booker Jr., and Alex for encouraging me to stay with it and to see it through.

I would like to thank my Sister - in - law, Gwen, for giving me her time and much needed feedback whenever asked. Finally, I would like to thank all my friends and family for giving me the inspiration to write again. My kids Marquise, Marchael, and Mariah are truly growing up before my eyes and I am committed to being a big part of their lives forever. I hope they can take a piece of this book and share it with their friends and classmates.

This country is going through a difficult time and everyone is looking for something good to hold on to and inspire them to keep on going no matter how hard the road may seem! This book is dedicated to all who believe in the American dream and the betterment of all people. We live in a Multi-Cultural society and this should be our greatest opportunity for global success. I hope you enjoy reading these motivational quotes, as much as I enjoyed writing them!

Michael A. Gunn

Table of Contents

"A good manager is one who can motivate people to do what they don't always want to do."

"The job won't make you miserable, but people who are miserable will."

WORKPLACE

"Work can be fun if you know how to make it that way."

"In business, we must learn to listen more and talk less."

WORKPLACE

"Always prepare for the worst when planning anything."

"Because many people allow their ego and pride to get in their way, much time and money is lost."

WORKPLACE

"In any business today,
the team must come first if the
goal is to be accomplished."

"The gift to teach is a gift rarely found."

WORKPLACE

"The customer will determine
how well you do in business
and how fast you'll fail."

"It takes time to become successful,
but it takes longer to be good at it."

WORKPLACE

"Take time to do things right the first time. Short cuts only cause delay in completing the goal."

"People will be your key to success in anything that you may do."

WORKPLACE

"Failure can be a very valuable learning lesson and an expensive one too."

"Black or White.
Democrat or Republican.
We all must work together for a common goal if we are to succeed as a nation."

WORKPLACE

"Planning ahead keeps us in tune for dealing with future problems."

"Corporations must learn that one doesn't save money by terminating people, but by changing the way they do business within the system."

WORKPLACE

"My success is your success."

DIVERSITY

"Black is powerful
White is powerful
So what's the problem?"

"Racism has inhibited our country's
growth, but more importantly, it will
keep us from being a world power."

"Racism starts at home and at an early age, so teach your children to love and not to hate, for they were God's children before they were yours."

"Racism unfortunately still exists and
shows its ugly face even in its
most inhabited places, but a human who
has an evil disposition toward another
simply because of the color of his
skin will doubtfully learn life
is too short to hate."

"To have faith is to believe."

"Faith, faith, faith. That's the only thing some people haven't enough of."

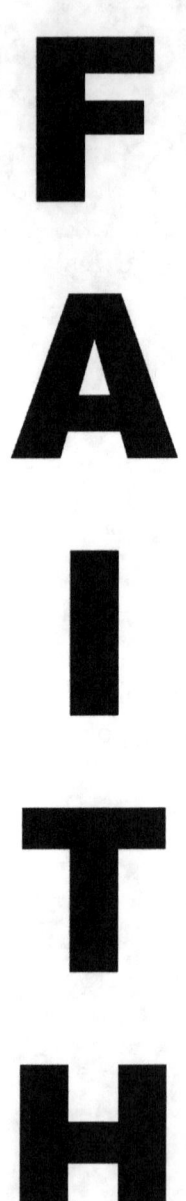

"To have talent in anything is a
blessing from above."

"Some preachers need to practice
what they preach."

"It's alright to thank God."

"Everyone should believe in a
higher power, for I believe in God."

"Have fun, because life is too short not to."

"Never belittle someone because of their lack of education, for they may be the one who builds your house and offer you a hand when no one else will."

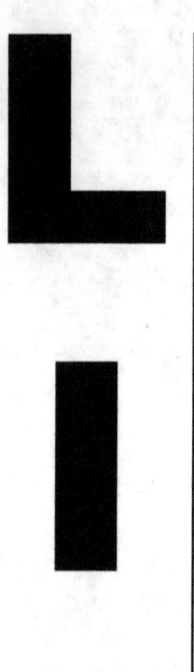

"Remain in control at all times, for control is one way to handle pressure."

"Be good to yourself."

"Know why something is."

"Treat yourself."

"Learn to trust someone."

"Be proud of who you are."

"Remember what your parents
taught you."

"Inquire, for all will not be stated
Persist, for no single thing is fated."

"Inspire others to strive for success."

"Learn the art of winning people's support. It may lead you to the White House."

"Some people need to learn
how to keep friends."

"It's hard to be different in a
society that promotes uniformity."

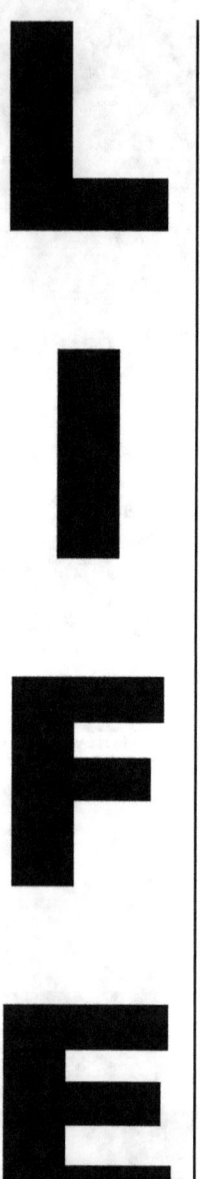

"Visualize what you want and go after it."

"Ask yourself – Why not me?"

"Everyone deserves at least a second
chance; it just might be you
the next time."

"Family should always come first."

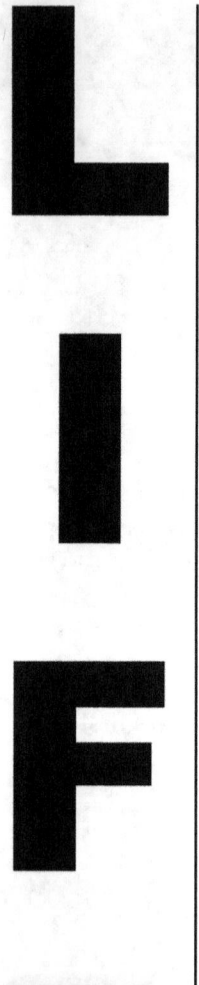

"Please do not text and drive, the life you save may be yours!"

"Sit back and take the time to reflect on the days of accomplishments."

"Sometimes the hospital is the only place some people can lose weight."

"Eat what you want, we will all die someday."

"Winning is fun, but losing is a
learning experience."

"Take action – make your
dreams a reality."

"Anyone can overcome their
fears if they allow themselves to
accept their realities."

"The most important time to maintain
your composure is when the odds
are stacked against you."

"People lie because they're unsure
from the start whether or not
their decision is right."

"Never give up on anything that you
want in life, and remember what
you have once you have it."

"Success in life will be determined
by how well you treat people."

"People who look for only the material
things in life will find that materials
can't bring happiness."

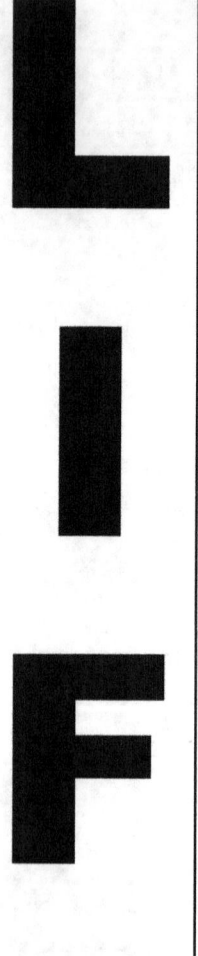

"Friends are easy to make, but are tough to keep."

"People don't readily remember the bad things they did, because no one likes to admit to doing others wrong."

"Never let negative thoughts play positive roles in your everyday life, for tomorrow is never promised."

"There will always be a time and a place where knowledge and experience can be used from the past."

"Life will have it's ups and downs, but it's up to us how down we get."

"Let the children show us how to learn and love."

"It's the children who can show us the way God intended us to be —not adults, for they think they know it all."

"Why is Christmas the only time people feel they must treat others with kindness and love? The world would be a better place if Christmas was every day."

"Too many people believe everything they read or see on television. This can be misleading. Truth can only be found by seeking it out for yourself."

"Always strive to get the best, look the best and be the best."

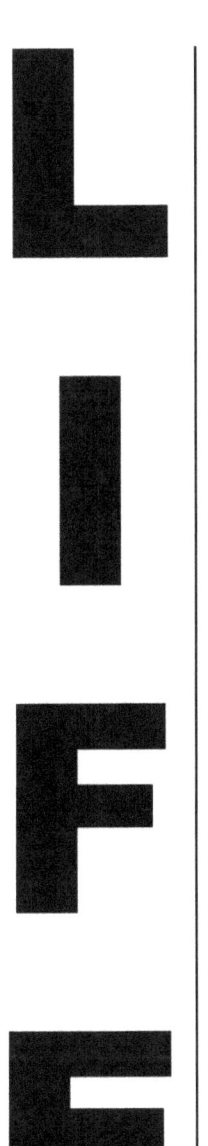

"Sometimes it's hard to please someone
no matter what you do."

"Beware of the person who tells
untruths and later denies it."

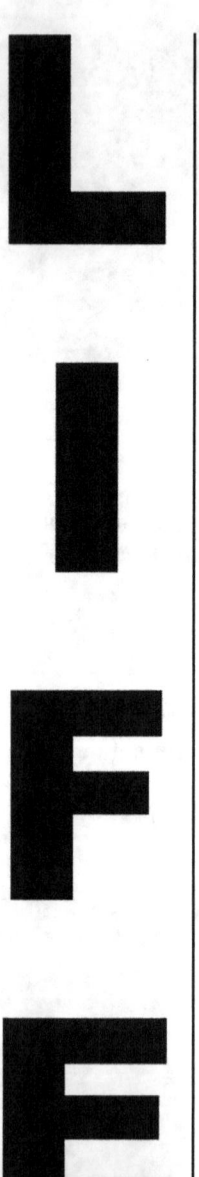

"Always be true to yourself."

"Keep in touch with the people you meet – they may lead you to success."

"Some people don't respect others because they don't respect themselves."

"Take time to relax and be with family and friends."

"It's alright to change your mind, but once the decision is made go with it all the way to the end."

"We must all make choices in life, the trick is not to make too many wrong ones."

"Be real."

"Freedom should be granted to everyone,
but no one should take it for granted."

"Politicians often make promises they can't keep, but the one who makes the least will surely not be reelected."

"Drugs won't just destroy your life, they'll erase it. People will forget who you once were."

"Education is the key to opening doors of opportunity. Knowing who has the keys is another matter."

"Always be aware of your environment for it's the environment that causes reasonable people to do irrational things."

"Anything man made is bound to have
problems for we are only human
and not perfect."

"Some people would do better without
any medicine at all."

"Life is not always fair
but never lose hope."

"Never give up on your dreams
and the challenges in life."

RELATIONSHIPS

"To show affection for someone when they have shown none for you says a lot about your character."

"Love should be from the heart and not the mind, because the mind can play tricks on you."

RELATIONSHIPS

"Anyone can have a relationship, but it's longevity will depend solely on how much one is willing to sacrifice and compromise their position."

"Men and women can learn a lot from each other – all it takes is someone to listen first."

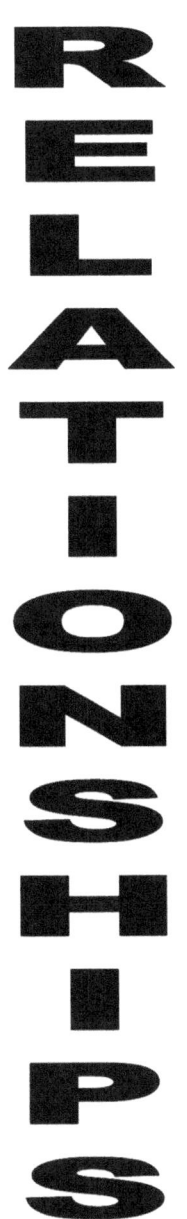

"All ladies like for men to send them roses, regardless of what they might say."

"If you love someone you must also trust them."

RELATIONSHIPS

" Sometimes people will say
I love you, only to get what
they want."

"When trying to win a woman's love one
needs not to give up easily, especially with
other competition. In life, we will always
compete for something, if not love."

RELATIONSHIPS

"Take time to listen.
Be able to forgive.
Never doubt one's feelings.
Show some sincerity.
Be able to remain friends.
Accept when it's over.
Allow time to heal.
Keep strong.
Do the right thing.
Grow from your mistakes.
Live."

FINI.

Words to Live By